DesignOriginals

NOTEBOOK DOODLES®
Sweets & Treats
Jess ♥ Volinski

YUM!

This book belongs to:

Design Originals

an Imprint of Fox Chapel Publishing
www.d-originals.com

Be Yourself to be creative

The thing I love most about art—making it myself or enjoying others' creations—is that **art allows you to be yourself by expressing yourself.** Whatever you love, whatever is important to you, whatever makes you who you are should come out in your art. By making art that matters to you, you're starting a conversation with everyone who sees it. You're saying, "Hey! This matters to me. What do **you** think about it?"

You might be wondering, how exactly do I express myself with art? That's where **The Elements of Art** come in. You might remember these from art class. Just like writers use words to tell a story, artists use these visual elements to express themselves and start their art conversation. All visual art—whether it is a painting in a museum, storyboards for a movie, a pattern on a bag, or a coloring book page—uses some combination of these seven basic building blocks of art. Not all art has to include all seven elements, but most art will include a few.

The Elements of Art

LINE

A **line** is formed as the connected distance between two points. Lines can be thick or thin, straight or curved.

SHAPE

A **shape** is a defined area of space—a circle, square, blob, or a flower petal are all shapes.

FORM

Something has **form** if it has volume (or creates the illusion of volume). A three-dimensional sculpture has form. A two-dimensional drawing with shading that makes it appear three-dimensional can also have form.

SPACE

Space refers to the areas in a piece of art that are around or within different parts of the art. There are two kinds of space: negative (space around areas), and positive (space within areas).

TEXTURE

Texture refers to the way the art physically feels when touched, or how an artist visually makes the art **look** like it would feel. Shading with pencils is an example of this type of visual texture.

COLOR

Color is created when light hits an object and is reflected to our eyes. A color can be described with three properties: hue (the color's name, such as "red"), value (how light or dark the color is, also called a tint or shade of the color), and intensity (how vivid or dull the color is).

VALUE

Value refers to the relationship between light areas and dark areas in a piece of art.

The Elements of art IN ACTION

Let's look at one of my doodles and see what Elements of Art are here. Even though this is just a simple black and white drawing, it has line, shape, and space. When you color it in, you'll probably add form, color, value, and maybe even texture. That's all seven Elements of Art—on a coloring book page! How cool is that?! Art truly is all around us!

Space (negative): The shape inside the curl is a negative space.

Shape

Line

Space (positive): The shape of this curl creates a positive space.

Texture

Form (and texture): The colored pencil texture makes the star look three-dimensional, giving it form.

Color

Value (dark)

Value (light)

Coloring Technique Ideas

Watercolors

Colored pencils layered over watercolors

Fine-point black pen layered over markers

Get inspired by COLOR

When it comes to expressing emotion, I think color is probably the most powerful Element of Art. To me, there's no better way to express how you're feeling, or how you want someone else to feel, than through the use of color. Just think of some of your favorite memories and how they make you feel. I bet color plays a big part of what you remember. Whether it's a beautiful sunset, the green of spring after a long, cold winter, or a perfectly clean, white expanse of snow, color makes a huge impact on us, both visually and emotionally. Just look at the way different colors can give the same flower drawing a completely different feel.

I've found that planning is key when working with color. If you're like me and you just **love** color, it might seem a bit overwhelming to get started. There are just so many color choices! And it's easy to fall into the rut of using the same colors over and over again, just because you like them. Making color decisions before you start can make you feel comfortable using new colors. Plus, you won't have to make a choice when you're in the midst of coloring and decide you don't like the result as much as you thought you would. A great way to try some new color combinations is to take a few minutes—it won't take long!—to create your own palettes before you get started.

Here's a fun trick I've learned for making palettes. It works especially well if you're using markers or colored pencils. Lay out all of your markers (or pencils) on a table or floor so you can see every single color you have. Pick one favorite marker (pencil) that will serve as the **anchor color** for your palette. Make it a color you really enjoy working with (or for a challenge, maybe a color you never work with). Now, pick two or three other markers (pencils) that complement your anchor color and place those next to your anchor color to start building a palette. Keep going until you have picked five or six colors. At this point, you don't even have to use them—you're just putting them side-by-side to see how the colors look together. Keep adding or switching colors until you like what you see. It's so easy to swap different colors in and out this way. Once you have a group of colors that you like, test them out on paper to make sure you still like the way they look together. If you love it, be sure to create a sample page with the names of the markers/colors you used so you won't forget. This is a great way to quickly create a whole library of color palettes for yourself.

Another great place to get color inspiration is literally from the world around you. Color is everywhere—your clothing, your bag, even a tissue box—there are probably patterns and designs with interesting color palettes surrounding you now! I'm sure there are things you bought because you liked the colors, so use those things that you love as inspiration. I once bought a pack of hair elastics simply because they had the most beautiful combination of blues and purples. Almost anything, anywhere, can become a color inspiration, so always keep your eyes open!

A SPECTRUM of Emotion

Color can be a great way to express yourself and define your mood. When you sit down to color, ask yourself, "How do I feel today? How can I use color to express that feeling?" Sometimes you might even feel something you can't quite put into words, but you can express it with color.

I've included some of my favorite palettes on the following page. Each one is paired with the emotion that best describes how the color combination makes me feel. But keep in mind that everyone is different, and that's what makes art so exciting. I love to use bright colors, but maybe you like more subdued colors. My "relaxed" palette might be your "cozy." There is no right or wrong when it comes to color! Use these palettes as a starting point and see how they make you feel. Try adding or taking away a color to customize the palette to reflect your taste and style. Then, make your own page full of YOUR favorite color palettes!

The next few pages contain some colored examples. You'll see two color palettes on each page, one at the bottom and one along the outer edge. The palette at the bottom shows the design's main colors in the large circles. The small circles show lighter colors (called tints) and darker colors (called shades) of those main colors. This is to give you the feeling of this palette and visually show which colors are dominant in the design (the bigger the circle, the more dominant the color).

Along the outer edge of each page, I've included a palette with each individual color, shown separately, so you can easily match your marker, pencil, or paint colors to the colors I used.

Whether you use one of my palettes or create your own, always be sure the colors you choose reflect who you are and how you're feeling.

Now go gather your art supplies—it's time to color!

The circles along the outer edge of the gallery pieces show you each individual color I used in that particular piece. If you like the palette I chose, you can use these circles to match the colors of your own pencils or markers.

The circles along the bottom of the gallery pieces show you which colors are more dominant in each design. The larger the circle, the more dominant the color. The smaller circles show tints and shades of a main color that were introduced for variety.

A SPECTRUM of Emotion

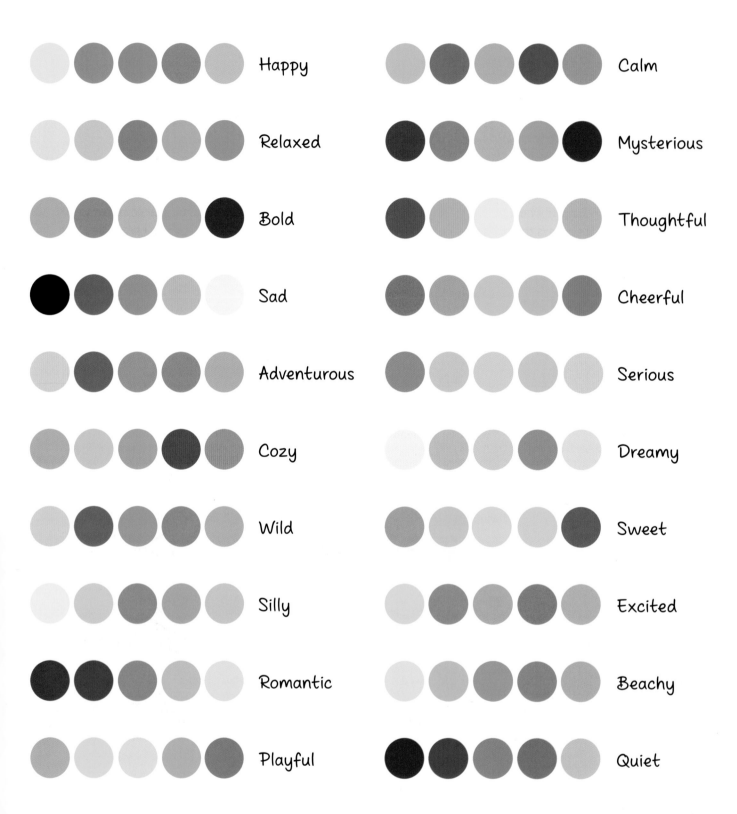

Happy

Relaxed

Bold

Sad

Adventurous

Cozy

Wild

Silly

Romantic

Playful

Calm

Mysterious

Thoughtful

Cheerful

Serious

Dreamy

Sweet

Excited

Beachy

Quiet

Take the COLOR WHEEL for a Spin!

A lot of times, simply following your feelings will lead you right to your color choices, but sometimes you might get stuck, and that's OK! Maybe you just don't know what you're feeling or you want to try something different with color and aren't sure where to start. The color wheel can be an awesome guide to help you make color choices.

The color wheel is a visual guide to the relationships between colors based on their position on the wheel. When placed together, certain colors look harmonious while others might clash. It all depends on the relationship of the colors to one another. Each color in a palette needs to be surrounded by the right companions to shine!

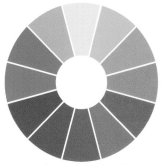

The Color Wheel

The color wheel diagrams below are a great starting place to find colors that will automatically look lovely together. But always remember, the color wheel is only a guide. Feel free to add more colors to a palette or take some away. The best color choices are always the ones that reflect how you're feeling and what makes you happy. Have fun!

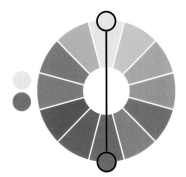

Complementary Colors
Complementary colors are pairs of opposites. They are directly across from one another on the color wheel.

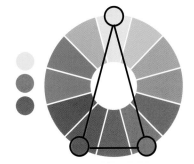

Split Complementary Colors
A split complementary color palette is created when one color is grouped with the two colors on either side of its complementary color.

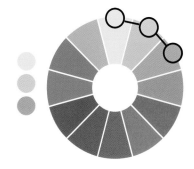

Analogous Colors
Analogous color palettes are created by choosing several colors that sit right next to each other on the color wheel.

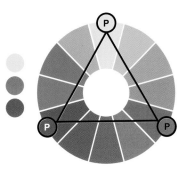

Primary Triadic Colors
Triadic means "group of three." The three primary colors (red, yellow, and blue) form a triadic palette when grouped together.

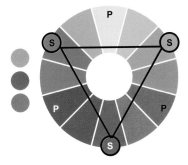

Secondary Triadic Colors
Secondary colors are the colors directly in between the primary colors on the color wheel. When you shift the triangle around the wheel by two spaces, you've found the secondary colors.

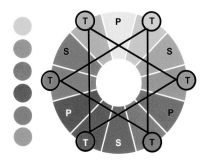

Tertiary Colors
Tertiary colors fall in between the primary and secondary colors. These are some of my favorite colors to work with!

Tetradic Colors
Tetradic means "group of four." Using a rectangle or square to choose colors on the color wheel is a fun way to instantly create a group of four colors that look great together. Both use two sets of complementary colors. Try rotating the rectangle or square around the wheel to create many different palettes.

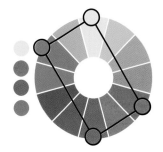

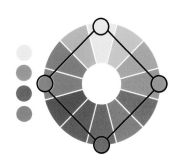

DONUT worry BE HAPPY

Choose **four** colors that are equally spaced around the color wheel in a **square** to make your own **tetradic** color palette!

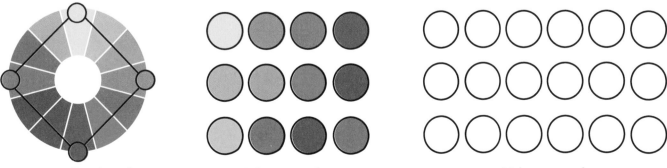

Square tetradic color palette

Palette examples

Make your own!
Also try adding a few additional colors.

Anything is good if it's
made of chocolate.

—Jo Brand

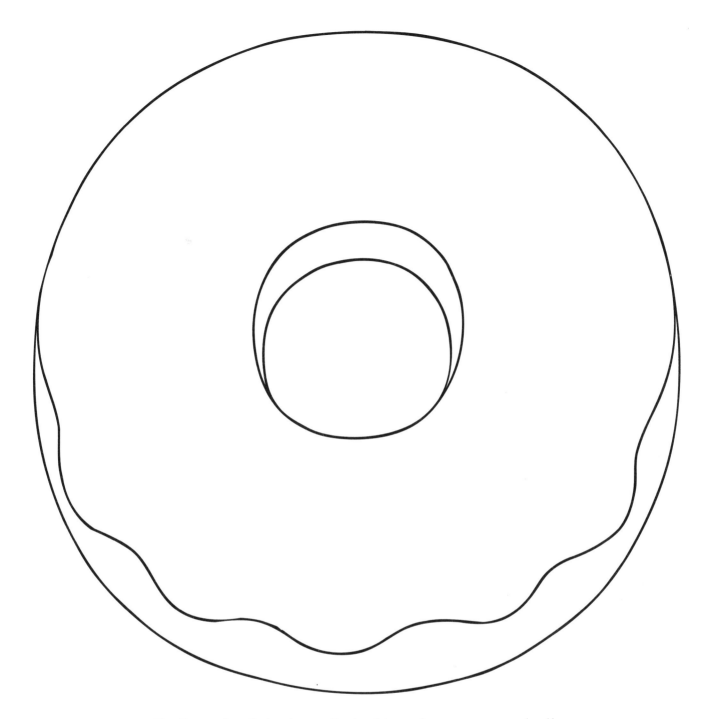

Doodle your favorite toppings on the donut to create your own yummy treat!

Choose four colors that are spaced around the color wheel in a **rectangle** to make your own **tetradic** color palette!

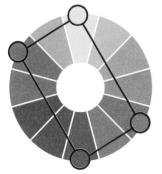

Rectangle tetradic color palette

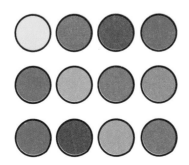

Palette examples

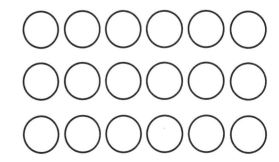

Make your own!
Also try adding a few additional colors.

The secret ingredient
is always love.

—Unknown

Choose **three colors** that are equally spaced from one another, making a triangle on the color wheel to create your own **triadic** color palettes!

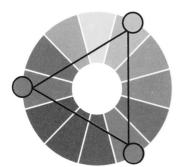

Triadic color palette

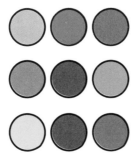

Palette examples

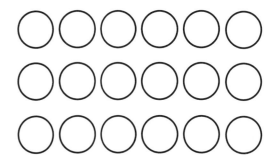

Make your own!
Also try adding a few additional colors.

If we are what
we eat, then I am
awfully sweet.

—Unknown

_____
_____
_____
_____
_____
_____
_____
_____
_____
_____

Design your own delicious cupcake.

Find a color you like and then choose the two colors right next to that color's complement to make your own **split complementary** color palette!

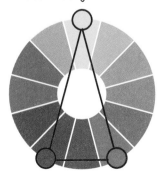

Split complementary colors

Palette examples

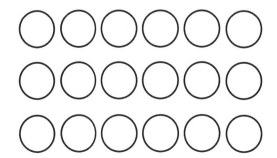

Make your own!
Also try adding a few additional colors.

Happiness is homemade.

—Unknown

Try choosing a palette of **3, 4, or 5 colors** that are right next to each other on the color wheel to make your own analogous color palettes!

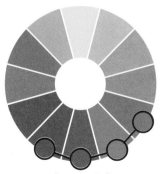

Analogous Colors

Palette examples

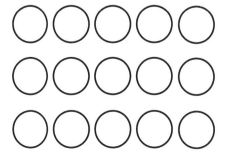

Make your own!
Also try adding a few additional colors.

Kindness is like sugar. It makes
life taste a little sweeter.

—Unknown

_____
_____
_____
_____
_____
_____
_____
_____
_____
_____

I could give up chocolate, but I'm no quitter!

—Unknown

you are so sweet

The best things in
life are sweet.

—Unknown

_____
_____
_____
_____
_____
_____
_____
_____
_____
_____

my Favorite treats

What are your ten most favorite, yummy treats?

All you need
is love. But a little
chocolate now and
then doesn't hurt.

—Charles M. Schulz

Candy makes life
just a little sweeter.

—Unknown

DONUT worry ♡ BE ♡ HAPPY

Life is short, and it is up to
you to make it sweet.

—Sarah Louis Delany

Everything in moderation, including moderation.

—Oscar Wilde

Add your own colorful frosting design to each cookie!

Nothing says home
like the smell of baking.

—Unknown

There is little in life
that could not benefit
from a little love, a little
time, and a little butter.

—Unknown

With enough butter,
anything is good.

—Julia Child

_____
_____
_____
_____
_____
_____
_____
_____
_____
_____

Laughter is brightest
where food is best.

—Irish proverb

Add your own delicious designs to the lollipops!

Everything tastes
better when you eat it
with friends.

—Unknown

_____

_____

_____

_____

_____

_____

_____

_____

_____

you're so **COOL**

It's never too
cold for ice cream.

—Unknown

_____

_____

_____

_____

_____

_____

_____

_____

_____

_____

_____

Dessert is like a
feel-good song, and the
best ones make you dance.

—Chef Edward Lee

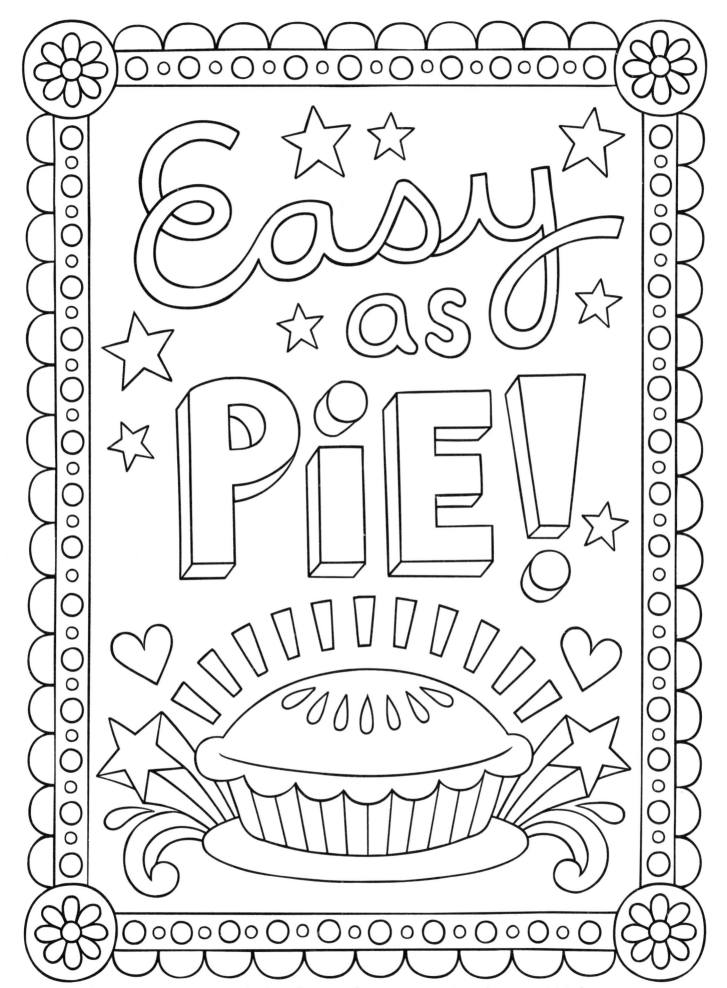

A balanced diet is having a
cupcake in each hand.

—Unknown

_____

_____

_____

_____

_____

_____

_____

_____

_____

Chocolate is the
answer—who cares
what the question is!

—Unknown

_____

_____

_____

_____

_____

_____

_____

_____

_____

_____

Dessert is so much
sweeter when shared
with good friends!

—Unknown

Life IS A PIECE of CAKE

Baking is love
made edible.

—Unknown

People who love to eat are always the best people.

—Julia Child

Add your favorite flavors of ice cream to the cone, cup, and bowl. Don't forget the toppings!

Life is better with
sprinkles on top.

—Unknown

_____
_____
_____
_____
_____
_____
_____
_____
_____
_____

Fill the jars with your favorite colorful candies!

Food for the body is not enough. There must be food for the soul.

—Dorothy Day

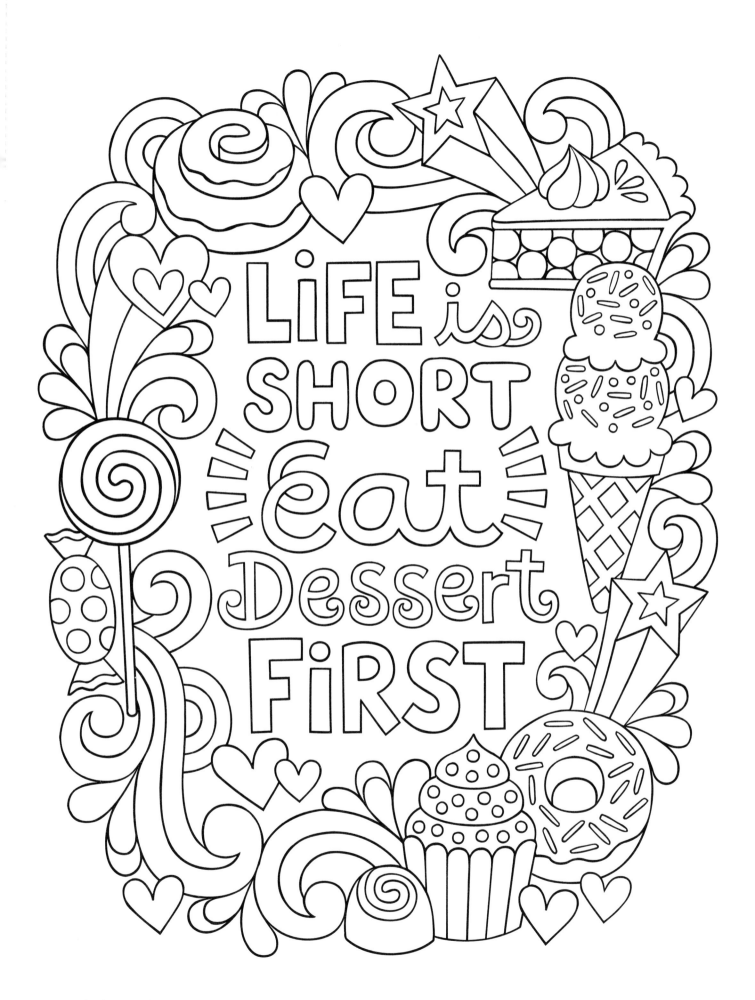

Indulge...life is sweet!

—Unknown

_____
_____
_____
_____
_____
_____
_____
_____

Enjoyment is an
incredible energizer to
the human spirit.

—John C. Maxwell

Happiness is knowing there
is cake in the oven.

—Unknown

_____
_____
_____
_____
_____
_____
_____
_____
_____

Now it's your turn! How would you decorate your own delicious cake?

A party without cake
is just a meeting.

—Julia Child

_____

_____

_____

_____

_____

_____

_____

_____

_____

_____

I've never met a
chocolate I didn't like.

—Unknown

_____
_____
_____
_____
_____
_____
_____
_____
_____
_____

Doodle, write about, or attach a picture of your dream dessert!

Never underestimate
the power of chocolate.

—Unknown

_____

_____

_____

_____

_____

_____

_____

_____

_____

_____

Absolutely
eat dessert first. The
thing that you want to
do the most, do that.

—Joss Whedon